Costa Rica Chica Cookbook

Stirring up my favorite North American recipes in Costa Rica

30 simple and delicious recipes for cooking in either Costa Rica or North America

FOR MOM:

For teaching me to peel an apple in one long curlicue,
for your patience when I was growing up and wanted NOTHING to do with cooking,
and for your pride in all my accomplishments; always.

Table of Contents

PREFACE

Once upon a time, my husband and I did this crazy thing – we quit our jobs in the good ole USA in our early 40's, sold virtually everything we owned, and moved to Costa Rica to live a more simple life with no stress and no regrets. It has become the best adventure of my life so far… .

Little did I know that Costa Rica would set my creative juices on fire. Among other things, I soon began to spend more and more time experimenting in the kitchen. I never made recipes from scratch before moving here. But now, making my own pie crusts, rustic bread, pizza crusts, tomato sauce – all from scratch – is so empowering to me.

There are some ingredients in the USA that you either cannot get here, that are slightly different, or that go by a different name completely. This cookbook has some of my favorite recipes I brought with me from North America which I have fine-tuned to incorporate the local ingredients found in Costa Rica. For those of you in the States – don't despair; this book also includes the original ingredients for you to use at home.

As Julia Child would say, "Bon Appetite!"

And as I say, "Que Rico!"

A WORD ABOUT WINE

Most people pair wines with their prepared foods at the dinner table. Nobody talks about what wines to pair with the *actual work* that goes into baking and cooking.

I'm here to tell you which wines go with each part of the cooking/baking process (yes, for you, the chef!) while you work in your kitchen:

Chopping – Chardonnay
Mixing - Merlot
Slicing – Sauvignon Blanc
Caramelizing - Cabernet Sauvignon

Mix and match the above as you see fit.

In Costa Rica, I highly recommend enjoying your wine in boxed form (Uvita and Clos are my favorites; both come in 1-liter boxes).

1. BREAKFAST

Breakfast Casserole

This is perfect for making a day ahead of time. Just refrigerate overnight, and the next morning, pop it in the oven – voilá! Breakfast is served.

Makes: 9 x 13-inch pan

INGREDIENTS

- 1 pound uncooked pork breakfast sausage or any type of meat/sausage
- 5 1/2 cups (approximately) French or sourdough baguette, cut into 3/4-inch cubes (or my No-Knead Rustic Bread or day-old bread is a good option)
- 12 large eggs
- 1 1/2 cups whole milk
- 1 small box **crema dulce** stored at room temperature (USA substitution = 1 cup of half and half cream)
- 1 teaspoon salt
- 1 teaspoon freshly ground black pepper
- 2 teaspoons Italian seasoning
- 1 teaspoon garlic salt
- 3/4 cup shredded mozzarella cheese
- 3/4 cup shredded cheddar cheese (plus some to sprinkle on top)

INSTRUCTIONS

1. Fry the sausage; break into pieces. Remove the pan from the heat and let it cool.
2. Place the eggs in a large bowl and whisk until they are blended. Add the milk, *crema dulce*, salt, pepper, Italian seasoning and garlic salt; and whisk to combine. Add the cheeses and combine. Set aside.
3. Spread the bread cubes in a 9 x 13-inch baking dish evenly. Spread sausage evenly on top of the bread.
4. Pour the liquid egg mixture over bread and meat, and sprinkle some additional shredded cheddar cheese on top. Cover the dish with plastic wrap or aluminum foil and refrigerate overnight.
5. When ready to bake the casserole, preheat the oven to 375° Fahrenheit (190° Celsius) and arrange a rack in the middle. Meanwhile, remove the casserole from the refrigerator and let it sit at room temperature (while the oven preheats).
6. Uncover the casserole and bake until a toothpick inserted into the center comes out clean, 35 – 45 minutes. Remove the pan to a wire rack and let it cool for 5 minutes before serving.

Cinnamon Coffee Cake

My pal Kathy sent me this recipe when I was in a pinch one day. "Jen's Bake Shop" was up and running, and I found myself a bit overwhelmed when a customer requested a coffee cake at the last minute. This recipe is easy and delicious, and is now my "go-to" coffee cake!

Makes: 9 x 13-inch pan

INGREDIENTS

Cake
- 2 eggs
- 2 teaspoons vanilla
- 1 cup sugar
- 3 cups flour
- 1 1/2 cups milk
- 1/4 teaspoon salt
- 4 teaspoons baking powder
- 1/2 cup butter (1 stick), melted

Cinnamon Swirl Layer
- 1 cup (2 sticks) butter, softened
- 1 cup brown sugar
- 2 tablespoons flour
- 1 tablespoon cinnamon

Glaze
- 1/4 – 1/2 cup powdered sugar
- 1 teaspoon vanilla
- milk (enough to make it the right consistency)

INSTRUCTIONS

1. Preheat oven to 350° Fahrenheit (176° Celsius).
2. Mix all cake ingredients. Pour into a greased 9 x 13-inch pan.
3. For the cinnamon swirl layer, mix the ingredients together until well combined. Drop evenly over the batter and swirl with a knife.
4. Bake for 28-35 minutes or until a toothpick comes out clean.
5. Once cake has cooled, whisk the powdered sugar with vanilla and enough milk to a thick consistency, but runny enough to drizzle. I like using a small plastic sandwich bag with the corner snipped off to drizzle the glaze diagonally over the whole cake.

Cream Drop Scones

This is the easiest scone recipe you will find! Some may call this a "short cut" recipe, but not me. These are just like real scones – slightly harder on the outside, and cake-y on the inside. OH YUM. I love scones!

Makes: 1 dozen

INGREDIENTS

Scones
- 1 1/3 cups all-purpose flour
- 2 tablespoons sugar
- 1 1/2 teaspoons baking powder
- 1/4 teaspoon salt
- 1 small box **crema dulce** stored at room temperature (USA substitution = 1 cup of heavy whipping cream)

Glaze
- 1 cup powdered sugar
- 1 1/2 tablespoons milk
- coarse sugar, for sprinkling (optional)

INSTRUCTIONS

1. Preheat the oven to 400° Fahrenheit (204° Celsius).
2. In a medium bowl, stir together the flour, sugar, baking powder and salt. Add the *crema dulce* and stir just until the dough comes together.
3. Drop by large spoonfuls onto a greased or parchment-lined (or a silicone mat) baking sheet.
4. Bake for 15-20 minutes or until golden.
5. Make the glaze by whisking the powdered sugar and milk together until it is the consistency you want. I like using a small plastic sandwich bag with the corner snipped off to drizzle the glaze.
6. Once the scones have cooled slightly, drizzle with the glaze and sprinkle with the coarse sugar. Serve and get ready for oohs and ahhs.

Chocolate Cream Cheese Banana Bread

How can you go wrong with chocolate, cream cheese, and bananas? Enough said.

Makes: 5 x 9-inch loaf pan (or three 3.5 x 7-inch loaf pans)

INGREDIENTS

- 1 stick (1/2 cup) unsalted butter, at room temperature
- 1 cup sugar
- 2 large eggs
- 1 1/4 cups all-purpose flour (NOTE: high altitude of 4,000 feet or more – add a bit more flour, about 2-3 tablespoons)
- 1/4 cup natural unsweetened cocoa powder
- 1 teaspoon baking soda
- 1 teaspoon salt
- 1 cup mashed very ripe bananas, approximately 3 large bananas
- 4 ounces **queso crema** (USA substitution = cream cheese)
- 1 teaspoon vanilla
- 1/2 cup semi-sweet chocolate chips (I've used milk chocolate in a pinch, and it is equally good)

INSTRUCTIONS

1. Preheat the oven to 350° Fahrenheit (176° Celsius). Grease a 3 x 5 x 9-inch loaf pan with non-stick cooking spray.
2. In a large bowl or electric mixer fitted with the paddle attachment, beat the butter and sugar until light and fluffy, 2-3 minutes.
3. Add the eggs one at a time, incorporating well after each addition.
4. Add the flour, cocoa powder, baking soda and salt. Beat gently until just combined.
5. Add the bananas, *queso crema* and vanilla and mix on low speed to combine.
6. Fold in the chocolate chips. Do not over mix.
7. Pour the batter into the prepared loaf pan and spread evenly with a spatula. Bake until a toothpick inserted into the center comes out with a few moist crumbs attached, about 60 – 70 minutes.
8. Note: If using three small loaf pans (3.5 x 7-inch), bake for 40-50 minutes.
9. Let the loaf rest in the pan for about 10 minutes, then turn it out onto a rack to cool completely.

Homemade Cinnamon Rolls

Greg says: "GOOD GOD, I'm going to have to go for another hike to burn off these calories!" These are seriously delicious. Also, in Costa Rica you cannot find commercially packaged pre-made cinnamon rolls, and even if you could, these are better.

Makes: 9 x 13-inch pan (12 large rolls)

INGREDIENTS

Dough
- 1 cup warm milk
- 1 egg (beaten)
- 1/4 cup butter, melted
- 1/4 cup vegetable oil
- 1/2 cup white sugar
- 1/2 teaspoon salt
- 3 1/2 cups flour
- 2 1/4 teaspoons yeast

Cinnamon Filling
- 1/2 cup (1 stick) butter room temperature
- 1/2 cup sugar
- 1/2 cup brown sugar
- 3 tablespoons cinnamon

Frosting
- 4 tablespoons (or more) **queso crema** (USA substitution = cream cheese) softened
- 1 1/2 cups powdered sugar
- 1 tablespoon milk (or cream)
- vanilla (a little, if desired)

INSTRUCTIONS

1. In a stand-mixing bowl, add milk, egg, melted butter, oil, sugar, and salt. Add flour on top of all the liquid mixture sprinkling yeast on top. Using the dough hook, knead bread mixture on speed 1 until dough is smooth and elastic, adding additional flour as needed (approximately 5-7 minutes).
2. Leave dough in bowl and cover with a towel. Allow the dough to rise in a warm area until doubled in size, (approximately 1 hour, depending on elevation).
3. In a small bowl, combine sugar, brown sugar, and cinnamon. Set aside.
4. When dough has risen, turn dough onto a lightly floured surface and roll into a rectangle slightly larger than a 9 x 13-inch rectangle. Spread surface evenly with soft butter with a knife. Sprinkle sugar mixture evenly all over the top. Starting with the long side, gently roll up. This will result in creating a log that will be cut into rolls. Use flour on your fingers if it gets too sticky.
5. I have found the absolute BEST way to cut the cinnamon rolls is with DENTAL FLOSS. Cut a 12" piece of floss, put the center of the floss underneath the roll where you want to cut it, and quickly criss-cross the ends of the floss on top of the roll all the way through to make a clean cut. Cut 12 equal slices in this way, and place them in a greased 9 x 13-inch baking pan, slightly spaced one inch apart from each other (they will rise). *(CONTINUED ON NEXT PAGE.)*

6. Spray a large piece of plastic wrap with cooking spray and cover loosely (sprayed side down), and allow to rise for 30 minutes.
7. (At this point, after 30 minutes of rising, you can refrigerate the rolls overnight up to 24 hours. Keep the plastic wrap on top. Take rolls out of fridge the next morning, remove the plastic wrap and let stand at room temperature for about 1 hour before baking as directed below).
8. Bake at 375° Fahrenheit (190° Celsius) for 25-30 minutes until golden brown and a toothpick inserted comes out clean. For even browning, check at 25 minutes to see if pan needs turning.
9. For frosting, cream the *queso crema* with a spatula (or stand mixer) until smooth. Add in the powdered sugar, milk and vanilla. Beat until smooth, creamy and thick. Spread over cinnamon rolls and serve immediately.

2. SOUPS

Tomato Basil Soup

Warning - this soup is addicting. It honestly tastes like La Madeleine's, creamy and so flavorful. Fresh basil is best. MUST eat with my No-Knead Rustic Bread for dipping!

Servings: 12 mug size cups

INGREDIENTS

- 8-10 medium/large sized tomatoes – blanched*, peeled and cored
- 1 tablespoon minced garlic
- 1 small can of **Maggi's Pasta de Tomate** (USA substitution = 1 small can tomato paste)
- 4 cups water
- 14 large basil leaves, plus more for garnish (substitute: 2.5 – 3 tablespoons dried basil)
- 1 small box **crema dulce** stored at room temperature (USA substitution = 1 cup of refrigerated heavy whipping cream)
- 1/4 – 1/2 cup cream cheese (optional – this makes it even more creamy)
- 1 stick unsalted butter (I have used ½ stick before, still good)
- 2 teaspoons cracked black pepper
- 1 teaspoon salt (to taste)
- to serve: parmesan cheese, basil leaves, pepper and No-Knead Rustic Bread

INSTRUCTIONS

1. Combine the tomatoes, garlic, Maggi's, water and basil leaves in a large saucepan.
2. Bring to a boil, then cover and simmer on low heat for 30 minutes.
3. After 30 minutes, add the *crema dulce*, cream cheese (if using), butter, pepper and salt. Cover and heat for 10 minutes.
4. Remove from heat, puree with a hand-held immersion blender. (If you do not have one, cool soup slightly and puree in batches in a blender.)
5. Garnish with grated parmesan, basil leaves, and pepper and enjoy with a hot loaf of my No-Knead Rustic Bread.

NOTE: This soup freezes well.

* Blanching tomatoes: Cut out top stems and cut a cross pattern on the bottoms of each tomato. Drop into a large pot of boiling water for 10-20 seconds, scoop out and put in ice bath for 10 seconds or so. Use a knife to peel the skin off – it will come off very easily.

Slow Cooker Baked Potato Soup

This soup is hearty and creamy – and tastes exactly like a baked potato! A meal in itself, and don't forget the cheddar cheese for the garnish.

Servings: 12 mug size cups

INGREDIENTS

- 20 baby potatoes – skin on, washed and cut into quarters (about 8 – 9 cups)
- 1 medium onion – finely diced
- 5 ½ cups chicken broth
- 1 teaspoon salt (or to taste)
- 2 teaspoons ground black pepper (or to taste)
- 1 small box **crema dulce** stored at room temperature (USA substitution = 1 cup of heavy whipping cream or 1 cup evaporated milk)
- 1/3 cup (5.33 tablespoons) butter
- 1/3 cup all-purpose flour
- 1/2 cup **natilla** (USA substitution = ½ cup sour cream) (optional)
- to serve: shredded cheddar cheese, **natilla**, bacon and chives

INSTRUCTIONS

1. In a large slow cooker, add potatoes, onion, chicken broth, salt and pepper and *crema dulce* or evaporated milk.
2. Cover with lid and cook on HIGH heat for 4 hours or LOW heat for 9 hours.
3. Once potatoes are soft, ladle out 2 cups liquid from soup mixture in crock pot into a liquid measuring cup, set aside.
4. In a medium saucepan, melt butter over medium heat. Add flour and cook for 2 minutes, stirring constantly. While whisking, slowly pour 2 cups liquid in measuring cup into butter mixture (it will thicken quickly). Pour butter mixture into slow cooker and stir to blend.
5. Mash potatoes with a potato masher to break down into smaller pieces or use an immersion blender to puree. Taste to see if you need more salt or pepper.
6. Cover and cook on HIGH heat until thickened, about 10 minutes. Turn heat off (or to low to keep warm), stir in *natilla*.
7. Garnish with shredded cheese, *natilla*, bacon and chives. Enjoy!

Broccoli Cheese Soup

This tastes amazingly like a certain restaurant's Broccoli Cheese Soup – especially when served in a "crock-bowl" on Fridays. I dare you to try to have just one small cup of this.

Servings: 8 mug size cups

INGREDIENTS

- 4 cups chicken broth
- 1 cup water
- 1 small box **crema dulce** stored at room temperature (USA substitution = 1 cup half and half or heavy whipping cream)
- 4 slices cheddar cheese singles (USA substitution = 4 slices of Cheddar Cheese Singles or American Cheese Singles) (confession: sometimes I add more than 4 slices)
- 1/2 cup all-purpose flour
- 1 teaspoon ground black pepper
- 4 cups broccoli florets (chopped into very small pieces)
- 1 small onion, diced
- to serve: shredded cheddar cheese and minced fresh parsley

INSTRUCTIONS

1. Combine chicken broth, water, *crema dulce*, cheese, flour and pepper in a large saucepan. Whisk to combine and to break up any lumps of flour, then turn heat to medium/high.
2. Bring soup to a boil, then add broccoli and onion and reduce heat to low. Cover and simmer for 25 - 30 minutes or until broccoli is tender but not too soft.
3. For each serving, ladle into a bowl and garnish with a heaping spoonful of shredded cheese and a pinch of parsley.

Chicken Enchilada Soup

A soup so hearty, it is truly a meal in itself. This is Greg's FAVORITE soup - ever. A bit of Mexico in our Costa Rican diet.

Servings: 8 mug size cups

INGREDIENTS

- 4 tablespoons vegetable oil
- 1 small onion, diced
- 1 garlic clove, diced or pressed
- 1 teaspoon ground cumin
- 1 teaspoon chili powder
- 1 teaspoon granulated garlic
- 1/4 teaspoon cayenne pepper
- 4 cups water
- 1 cup **masa harina** *
- 4 cups chicken broth
- 3 medium tomatoes, seeded and chopped
- 7 - 8 slices American cheese
- 2 - 3 cooked and shredded chicken breasts
- to serve: tortilla chips, shredded cheddar cheese

INSTRUCTIONS

1. Add the oil to a large pot over medium heat. Add onions, garlic, cumin, chili powder, granulated garlic and cayenne pepper to the pot and sauté, stirring occasionally, until onions are soft and translucent, about 3-5 minutes.
2. In bowl, combine the *masa harina* with the 4 cups of water. Whisk until all lumps dissolve. Add to the pot of onions/garlic and bring to a boil.
3. Once it starts to bubble, cook for 2 to 3 minutes, stirring constantly, until it thickens.
4. Stir in the chicken broth and chopped tomatoes and let the soup return to a boil, stirring occasionally.
5. Add the cheese and chicken; then reduce heat, cover, and simmer for 30-40 minutes.
6. Serve soup in cups or bowls, and garnish with a large handful of crumbled tortilla chips and shredded cheddar cheese.

* *Masa harina* is a very finely ground corn flour. Mixed with water or oil, it forms the dough called *masa* that is used to make corn tortillas. This is easily found everywhere in Costa Rica but can also be found in the USA.

Chicken Tortilla Soup

This is a healthy broth soup (finally – no cream!). The limóns and avocado make this soup so flavorful and tasty – even Greg loves it. Don't tell him it's "healthy."

Servings: 8 mug size cups

INGREDIENTS

- 1 tablespoon olive oil
- 1 onion, chopped and diced
- 2 *jalapeños*, seeded and minced
- 6 cloves garlic, minced
- 7 cups chicken broth
- 1 cup of water
- 2 medium tomatoes, seeded and diced
- 1 teaspoon ground cumin
- Salt and freshly ground black pepper, to taste
- 4 small (or 2 double-breasted) boneless, skinless chicken breasts
- 1/3 cup chopped cilantro
- 4 tablespoons freshly squeezed **limón** juice (USA substitution = lime juice)
- to serve: diced avocados, tortilla chips, monterey jack cheese (or similar), and **natilla** (USA substitution = sour cream)

INSTRUCTIONS

1. In a large pot, heat olive oil over medium heat. Once hot, add onions and *jalapeños*, sauté until tender, about 2 minutes. Add garlic during last 30 seconds of sautéing.
2. Add chicken broth, water, tomatoes, cumin, salt and pepper to taste, and chicken breasts. Bring mixture to a boil over medium high heat. Then reduce heat to medium, cover with lid and allow to cook, stirring occasionally, until chicken has cooked through 10 - 15 minutes. Cook time will vary based on thickness of chicken breasts.
3. When chicken is done, reduce burner to low heat, remove chicken from pan and shred, then return chicken to soup.
4. Stir in cilantro and *limón* juice. Taste (see if you need more seasoning or *limón* juice).
5. To serve, add a dollop of *natilla*, diced avocados, crumbled tortilla chips and shredded cheese.

3. PIZZAS & BREADS

No-Knead Rustic Bread

Who wants to knead bread all day? Not me! I love this recipe – it is easy and it truly makes the BEST bread. This is a beautiful artisan style loaf, which is crusty on the outside and soft and airy on the inside.

Servings: 4 small loaves

INGREDIENTS

- 6 1/4 cups flour
- 1 1/2 tablespoons salt
- 1 1/2 tablespoons yeast
- 3 cups warm water

INSTRUCTIONS

1. In a large re-sealable plastic container (mine is 6" high and 9" diameter) add flour with salt and yeast sprinkled on top. Add 3 cups warm water and stir with a wooden spoon until a loose, sticky dough forms. When there are no more pockets of unmixed flour or water left, put a towel over the top of the container, and let the dough sit at room temperature until it doubles in size (I let mine rise 6 hours).
2. When the dough has risen, fit the lid onto the container and seal it. Place the container in the fridge for a few hours, or overnight. This dough will keep in the fridge for 3 weeks. (I've also taken some dough at this point and baked it right away, but it is easier to work with if you refrigerate for at least a couple of hours.)
3. Preheat your oven for 30 minutes at 450° Fahrenheit (232° Celsius) with a covered Dutch oven* inside. Scoop out a hunk of the dough (grapefruit size). Turn dough in hands, gently stretching surface of dough, rotating ball a quarter-turn as you go, creating a rounded top and pinch bottom together. Set out on floured surface, sprinkle a bit of flour on top, and cover with towel for 30 minutes while the oven preheats.
4. When the oven is preheated, using a serrated knife, slash top of dough in three parallel, 1/4-inch deep cuts. Flour your hands and place dough in hot Dutch oven, cover, and bake for 30 minutes. Uncover and bake for 10 – 20 minutes more (time depends on your oven – you want it nice and crusty on top when done.)

* NON-Dutch oven way: You can make a "faux-Dutch oven" by using a metal pie plate and make a "tented" aluminum foil cover (you will need room for the dough to rise while it bakes). Bake with the instructions above (removing foil cover after 30 minutes). The secret of the Dutch oven (faux or real) is that it traps the moisture inside the loaf when it first begins to bake, giving it the air pockets and chewiness that is so delectable.

Garlic Cheddar Beer Bread Muffins

These are perfect to eat with corn chowder or chili. Or just by themselves. My friend Lynette has sprinkled crispy crumbled bacon on top as well, which makes them even MORE over-the-top wonderful.

Servings: 18 regular sized muffins

INGREDIENTS

- 3 cups flour
- 2 tablespoons sugar
- 4 teaspoons baking powder
- 1 teaspoons salt
- 1 teaspoons garlic salt
- pinch of cayenne pepper
- 1 cup shredded cheddar cheese (plus more to sprinkle on top)
- 8 tablespoons melted butter
- 1 bottle of **Imperial Beer** (USA substitute = any beer of your choosing)
- 4 tablespoons melted butter

INSTRUCTIONS

1. Preheat oven to 350° Fahrenheit (176° Celsius). Spray muffin tins with cooking spray.
2. In a bowl combine the flour, sugar, baking powder, salt, garlic salt, cayenne pepper and cheese. Stir until well mixed.
3. Pour in the 8 tablespoons of melted butter plus the beer. Stir until just combined.
4. Pour batter into muffin tins until each well is about 1/2 full. Pour remaining 4 tablespoons of butter onto the tops of the muffins, dividing evenly between each muffin. Top with additional cheese.
5. Bake for 20-25 minutes or until the muffins have puffed, the tops are slightly brown and a toothpick in the center comes out clean. I like to broil these for the last 3 minutes to get nice and crispy on top.

NOTE: If you are doing mini-muffins: bake for about 15-18 minutes (again, broil for last 3 minutes for a crispy, brown top).

Thin Crust Pizza

If you like thin crust pizza, you must try this recipe. Light and crispy and totally satisfying.

Servings: 2 pizza crusts

INGREDIENTS

- 3 cups flour
- 2 teaspoons yeast
- 1/4 teaspoon salt
- 1/2 tablespoon olive oil
- 1 cup warm water (may need a bit more – but start with 1 cup)

INSTRUCTIONS

1. Add all of the above ingredients (in the order listed) in a stand-mixer mixing bowl. Mix by hand with dough hook until just combined.
2. Attach bowl and dough hook, and set to slow speed. After about 30 seconds, a ball should form. At this point, either add water (if dough is too dry and not combining) or flour (if it's sticking to sides). After it starts forming a ball properly, allow mixer to knead for 8 minutes (slow speed). (Note: after 8 minutes, sometimes the "ball" becomes more goopy and the dough is more spread out, all is still fine!).
3. On a floured surface, divide dough in two. Shape into a *boule* shape (resembling a squashed ball, the typical rustic loaf shape), sprinkle with flour, cover with towel. Let rise for 45-55 minutes.
4. (NOTE: At this point, after rising, you can spray the insides of a plastic ziplock bag with cooking spray, place dough inside, seal and place in freezer for use at a later date. To thaw, put in refrigerator overnight, and then let rest on counter for 30 minutes with flour sprinkled on top and towel to cover.)
5. Work dough into a circle, then use knuckles to shape, letting gravity do its work or use rolling pin to roll out and shape (I tend to use the rolling pin). Brush 2 pizza pans with oil, cooking spray or corn meal. Press dough across bottom of pan forming a collar around edge to hold filling. Top with fillings.
6. Preheat oven for 30 minutes at 500° Fahrenheit (260° Celsius) (I start preheating the oven when the dough is in its last 30 minutes of rising). Bake pizza for 10-12 minutes (check after 10 minutes).

TO PARBAKE: Bake crusts at 450° Fahrenheit (232° Celsius) for 3 minutes, let cool, add toppings, freeze. After they are frozen solid, wrap in plastic wrap, and then aluminum foil to keep in freezer. To bake: set out at room temperature for 30 minutes while oven preheats to 500° Fahrenheit (260° Celsius), then bake for 8-9 minutes or until done.

Crack Bread

This stuff. You guys. Try to not eat the whole loaf in one sitting.

Servings: 1 loaf

INGREDIENTS

- 1 crusty loaf of Rustic Bread (from the No-Knead Rustic Bread recipe)
- 7 tablespoons butter
- 1/2 teaspoon garlic salt
- 1/2 teaspoon salt
- 1 tablespoon of your favorite herbs (parsley, dill, Italian seasoning, rosemary, *etc.*)
- 1 cup shredded cheddar cheese

INSTRUCTIONS

1. Preheat the oven to 350° Fahrenheit (176° Celsius).
2. Melt butter and then mix in salts and herbs/seasonings (not cheese).
3. Cut the whole loaf with diagonal slashes (but not through the bottom), and then cut with diagonal slashes the other way (forming 1" cubes throughout).
4. Place loaf on a large sheet of aluminum foil (enough to wrap sides up and over the loaf), and then on a baking sheet. Use your fingers or a knife to pry open each crack and drizzle in the butter/seasoning and then stuff in the cheese. This might sound like a bit of an effort, but I promise you it is worth it. You don't need to be super neat; some butter drizzled over the top of the crust will be delicious.
5. Wrap the loaf completely in foil and bake on cookie sheet for 15 minutes until the cheese has mostly melted; then unwrap and bake for 5 minutes more to make it brown and crusty.
6. Serve immediately.
7. You're welcome.

HINT: Don't be shy, experiment! Try ranch seasoning, bacon and cheese. For a morning treat, try a cinnamon and sugar combo with a cream cheese frosting drizzled on top.

Sweet Cornbread

Not your typical cornbread, this is sweet and will melt in your mouth. You will need a spoon or fork to eat this – but it is worth it.

Makes: 9 x 13-inch pan

INGREDIENTS

- 4 cups fresh or frozen (thawed) corn kernels
- 1/3 cup vegetable shortening
- 2 sticks unsalted butter, softened
- 2 cups corn **masa harina***
- 1/3 cup ice water
- 1/2 cup flour
- 3/4 cup sugar
- 1/4 cup **crema dulce** stored at room temperature (USA substitution = ¼ cup refrigerated heavy whipping cream)
- 1/2 teaspoon baking powder
- 1/2 teaspoon salt
- to serve: shredded cheddar cheese (optional)

INSTRUCTIONS

1. Preheat oven to 375° Fahrenheit (190° Celsius). Place the corn kernels in a processor and pulse the machine on and off, until mixture is coarsely chopped. Set aside.
2. Place vegetable shortening and butter in a mixing bowl and beat on medium high speed until light and fluffy. Add *masa harina* to butter mixture and mix for 2 minutes, until thoroughly incorporated. Add ice water and mix at medium for 1 minute or until completely absorbed.
3. In separate mixing bowl, combine flour, sugar, *crema dulce*, baking powder, and salt.
4. Add the *masa* mixture and ground corn to this flour/sugar mixture; stir to combine thoroughly. Pour batter into a prepared oiled (or sprayed) pan. Cover tightly with aluminum foil to retain the steam. Bake for 45 minutes.
5. Serve warm, dish onto a plate (you can use an ice cream scoop and form into a mound to be fancy), and sprinkle with shredded cheddar cheese if you like.

* *Masa harina* is a very finely ground corn flour. Mixed with water or oil, it forms the dough called *masa* that is used to make corn tortillas. This is easily found everywhere in Costa Rica but can also be found in the U.S.

4. THIS & THAT

Greg's HOT Beans

"Burns going in, burns going…", says Greg. Kidding. But these are a tad spicy. Remember - you don't have to make these as spicy as my Spice Monster husband does.

Makes: 6 cups

INGREDIENTS

- 1 cup of dry black beans
- 1 cup of dry red beans
- 5 cups water
- 1 small can of **Maggi's Pasta de Tomate** (USA substitution = 1 small can tomato paste)
- 2 garlic cloves, diced
- 1 *jalapeño*, finely diced
- 1 tomato, seeded and chopped
- 1 green pepper, chopped
- 1/2 teaspoon salt
- 1/2 teaspoon pepper
- 1/2 teaspoon Italian seasoning
- 1/2 teaspoon cumin
- 1/2 teaspoon garlic salt
- 1/2 teaspoon red pepper flakes (optional or more to taste)
- 1/4 teaspoon cayenne pepper (optional)
- 3 shakes hot sauce (optional or more to taste)

INSTRUCTIONS

1. In a large soup pan, bring all of the above ingredients to a boil on the stove. Then cover, turn to low and simmer for 6 hours.
2. And no, I do not soak my beans overnight or anything. Just toss them in and simmer for most of the day.

Jen's Salsa

Greg says he could drink my salsa, it's that good. Of course he likes it spicier than this recipe calls for, so just add more jalapeños, hot sauce, or red pepper flakes if you want it spicier too. Greg also loves this salsa because he thinks, "This is healthy for me, right?"

Makes: 6 cups

INGREDIENTS

- 6-7 or more tomatoes
- 4 cloves garlic
- 1/2 onion
- 1 red pepper
- 1 *jalapeño* or chili pepper *(NOTE: if you don't have this on hand, just use red pepper flakes or hot sauce)*
- small bunch of cilantro
- 1/2 **limón** – juice squeezed (USA substitution = juice of 1/2 of a lime)
- 1 teaspoon salt
- 1 teaspoon garlic salt
- 1/2 teaspoon cumin
- 1/2 teaspoon chili powder
- onion salt (to taste)
- pepper (to taste)
- Italian seasoning (to taste)
- red pepper flakes or hot sauce to taste

INSTRUCTIONS

Put everything in a blender and puree until smooth. You may need to do in batches, depending on how large your blender is.

Lemon-Ginger-Honey in a Jar

I swear this stuff has magical powers. I always make a cup when my stomach is upset, or my throat hurts – and it always makes me feel better. I really feel like this heads off that cold before it really hits.

Makes: about 1 cup

INGREDIENTS

- 1 **limón** (USA substitution = 1 lemon), thoroughly cleaned and thinly sliced
- 1 piece of ginger about the size of your thumb, skinned and sliced into coin size pieces
- honey (about 1/2 cup, maybe more)

INSTRUCTIONS

1. In a clean 6-ounce (or larger) mason jar, distribute lemon slices and ginger.
2. Pour honey over it slowly. This may take a few tries to let the honey sink down and around the *limón* and ginger slices. Make sure when the honey has filled in all the air pockets, there is enough to cover the top of the *limón* and ginger slices by a smidge.
3. Close jar and keep refrigerated. The mixture will form a loose sort of honey (it does not thicken).
4. When you want a cup of "lemon-ginger-honey (magical) tea," add a heaping spoonful (make sure you get at least one *limón* or ginger slice, the rest honey) to a mug, and pour 1 cup of boiling hot water over it and stir. Salud!

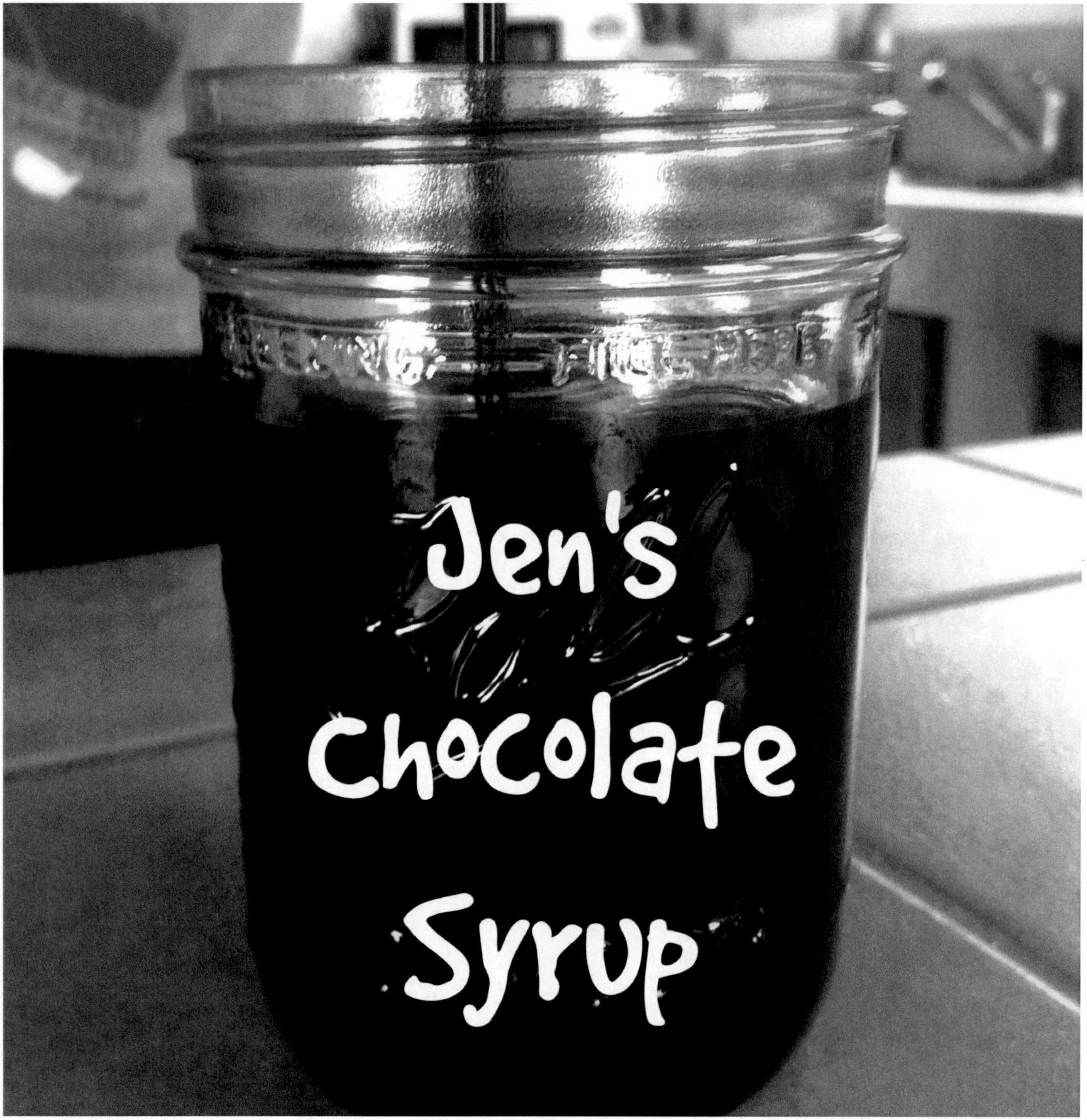
Jen's
Chocolate
Syrup

Jen's Chocolate Syrup

This makes a wonderfully thick syrup – excellent over ice cream or stir with milk to make chocolate milk. Very similar to Hershey's, but all homemade.

Makes: about 2 cups

INGREDIENTS

- 3/4 cup cocoa powder
- 1 1/4 cups water
- 1 1/2 cups sugar
- dash of salt
- 1 1/2 teaspoons vanilla extract

INSTRUCTIONS

1. In a large saucepan, combine the cocoa powder, water, sugar and salt over medium heat. Mix with a whisk until smooth.
2. Stir constantly with a whisk or a wooden spoon until it boils.
3. Allow it to boil for 3-4 minutes, whisking the whole time.
4. Remove from heat, and add vanilla.
5. Syrup will still be very thin. Allow to cool completely and it will thicken.
6. Store in a mason jar or any other container. It will keep for months in the fridge.

Chewy Granola Bars

I always make these because they just "feel" healthy, but really – I just can't keep them around that long. Better than a candy bar.

Makes: 12 bars

INGREDIENTS

- 3 cups **avena integral** (USA substitution = old-fashioned whole oats)
- 2 tablespoons oil
- 2 tablespoons brown sugar
- 2 tablespoons maple syrup
- 4 tablespoons (¼ cup) honey
- 1 teaspoon vanilla
- 1 teaspoon cinnamon
- 1/4 teaspoon nutmeg
- 1 – 1 1/2 cups add-ins (nuts, dried cranberries, raisins, chocolate chips, coconut, *etc.*)
- 5 ounces good dark chocolate

INSTRUCTIONS

1. Preheat the oven to 350° Fahrenheit (176° Celsius) and scatter the *avena integral* on a cookie sheet. You can include the nuts and coconut, if you want. Let them toast, stirring at least once, for about 15 minutes.
2. Line a 9 x 13-inch pan (or you can use a 9 x 9-inch pan if you want thicker bars) with parchment paper. You want a piece of parchment paper large enough that the long sides will come back over and cover the top of the bars once you fill the pan. Spray the parchment paper with cooking spray.
3. In small saucepan, heat the oil, brown sugar, maple syrup, honey, vanilla, cinnamon, and nutmeg. Bring it to a simmer over medium high heat. Stir to make sure the brown sugar dissolves, and remove from heat.
4. Put the toasted oats in a large bowl. Pour the hot liquid over the oats and stir to coat evenly. Stir in all your add-ins. Scrape the mixture into the prepared pan.
5. Fold the parchment over the top of the granola in the pan and PRESS DOWN to fill the corners and flatten. Keep pressing and smooth the granola out so that it is even across the pan.
6. Cool at room temperature for 2 to 3 hours, and then refrigerate for 20 minutes or so, before cutting into bars. (Correct – no cooking!)
7. Melt the chocolate in a small saucepan over low heat. Use a spoon to drizzle the chocolate over the sliced bars. Let it set up and enjoy! I like to store in the refrigerator – they still keep chewy!

5. HEARTY ENTREES

Chicken Enchiladas

My secret ingredient is queso crema (cream cheese), which makes everything taste better. I love making this when we have friends over. You can make ahead of time, keep covered in the fridge, and then bake when ready (add 5 minutes to the time below).

Makes: 9 x 13-inch pan

INGREDIENTS

- 8 ounces **queso crema** (USA substitution = cream cheese), softened
- 8 ounces shredded mozzarella (or similar) cheese, shredded
- 1/2 teaspoon cumin
- 1/2 teaspoon chili powder
- 1/4 teaspoon garlic salt
- 1/4 teaspoon onion powder
- 1/4 teaspoon pepper
- 2 cooked chicken breasts, shredded
- 8 -10 flour tortillas (7" – 8" size works best)
- cooking spray
- cheddar cheese (enough to sprinkle on top)
- fresh cilantro to garnish

Sauce
- 3 tablespoons butter
- 3 tablespoons flour
- 2 cups chicken broth
- 1 cup **natilla** (USA substitution = sour cream)

INSTRUCTIONS

1. Preheat the oven to 350° Fahrenheit (176° Celsius).
2. Stir together *queso crema*, mozzarella cheese and seasoning. Fold in chicken.
3. Divide among tortillas, roll up, place in sprayed 9 x 13-inch dish.
4. In a sauce pan over medium high heat, melt butter. Then stir in flour and whisk for 1 minute. Add broth and whisk until smooth. Heat over medium heat until thick and bubbly (about 4 minutes), whisking the whole time. Remove from heat, whisk in *natilla* until smooth.
5. Pour evenly over enchiladas. Add shredded cheese on top (cheddar is best!).
6. Bake for 25 minutes (then turn to broil for 3 minutes, if desired). Garnish with fresh cilantro and serve!

Baked Chicken Flautas

These are so yummy and delicious, and you will not even MISS the fact that they are not fried. Serve with salsa, guacamole or my Taco Dip.

Makes: 2 dozen

INGREDIENTS

- 2-3 chicken breasts, cooked and shredded
- fresh **limón** juice, squeezed from 2 **limónes** (USA substitution = lime juice)
- 1/4 teaspoon onion powder
- 1/4 teaspoon garlic powder
- 1 teaspoon cumin
- 1 teaspoon chili powder
- 4 tablespoons chopped cilantro
- 3/4 cup grated mozzarella, pepper jack or cheddar cheese
- salt and pepper, to taste
- 25 small flour tortillas (taco size)
- cooking spray or olive oil
- black pepper
- chili powder
- to serve: salsa, guacamole or my Taco Dip

INSTRUCTIONS

1. Preheat the oven to 425° Fahrenheit (218° Celsius) and line two baking sheets with silicone mats (or parchment paper).
2. In a large bowl, add the shredded chicken, *limón* juice and all seasonings, tossing to combine. Add cheese, and stir to combine.
3. Put tortillas in microwave for about 30 seconds or so – to warm a bit and make more pliable. Place about 2 tablespoons (not a lot – you want to keep these skinny) of chicken mixture on the lower third of a tortilla, keeping it about 1 inch from the edges. Roll up very tightly and place seam side down on a baking sheet, not touching one another (press down slightly, helps the form to hold). Spray lightly with cooking spray, or lightly brush with olive oil and sprinkle lightly with black pepper and chili powder. Place pan in oven and bake for 15-17 minutes or until crisp and the ends start to get golden brown. Remove from oven and let cool slightly before serving.
4. Freezer Instructions: After flautas are prepared and on baking sheets, place in the freezer and freeze until solid, then transfer to a large freezer bag. When ready to cook, preheat oven to 425° Fahrenheit (218° Celsius) and place the flautas on a lined baking sheet. Bake for 17-20 minutes or until golden brown and crispy.

Momma Beck's Wisconsin Lasagna

I have to thank my mom for passing down this cheesy lasagna recipe to me. And when I say cheesy, I mean CHEESY – this is from Wisconsin after all, ya know. My Texas husband always asks for this.

Makes: 9 x 13-inch pan

INGREDIENTS

- 2 pounds ground beef
- 1 small can of **Maggi's Pasta de Tomate** (USA substitution = 1 small can tomato paste)
- 4-5 medium tomatoes, finely chopped (or a can of chopped tomatoes, drained)
- 1 1/2 cups water
- 1 garlic clove, minced
- 2 teaspoons salt
- 2 teaspoons Italian seasoning
- 1 teaspoon black pepper
- lasagna noodles, cooked (at least 9, maximum 12)
- 8 ounces mozzarella shredded cheese
- 12 slices American cheese (the square shape that is individually wrapped)
- 4 ounces (or more) parmesan cheese

INSTRUCTIONS

1. Cook the ground beef in large/deep frying pan. Drain fat. Mix in Maggi's, tomatoes, water, and seasonings. Simmer for 30 minutes, covered.
2. Preheat the oven to 375° Fahrenheit (190° Celsius).
3. In a glass 9 x 13-inch pan, make 3 layers (or 4 layers if you have 12 noodles) of the following: 3 noodles next to each other, meat mixture, 4 slices of American cheese, sprinkle mozzarella cheese, sprinkle parmesan cheese. Repeat.
4. Bake for 30 minutes (uncovered), it should be very bubbly and just starting to turn brown on top, and your kitchen will smell wonderful. Cool 5 minutes before cutting.
5. You can also make ahead of time and keep in refrigerator (covered), then bake at 375° Fahrenheit (190° Celsius) for 35 minutes.

NOTE: Some say it is not really lasagna without ricotta cheese. For those of you who need a ricotta cheese layer, since ricotta is hard to find in Costa Rica, try this: use a combination of cream cheese, grated parmesan, shredded mozzarella, parsley, pepper, Italian seasoning and an egg to hold it all together. Experiment!

Costa Rican Stuffed Red Peppers

These are very similar to stuffed green peppers but are made with the red chile dulce (sweet peppers) that are prevalent here in Costa Rica.

Makes: 9 x 13 pan (12 halved and stuffed peppers)

INGREDIENTS

- 6 Costa Rican *chile dulce* peppers (these are sweet peppers, typically red, but should not be confused with the poblano peppers from Mexico which can be hot, although they have a similar shape) (USA substitution = bell peppers in any color - green, red, yellow or orange)
- 1 pound ground beef
- 1 small can of **Maggi's Pasta de Tomate** (USA substitution = 1 small can tomato paste)
- 1/2 cup uncooked rice
- 1 cup water
- 1/4 teaspoon oregano
- 1/4 teaspoon black pepper
- 1/2 teaspoon garlic powder
- 1/2 teaspoon cumin
- 1/2 teaspoon chili powder
- 1 cup shredded cheddar cheese
- to serve: ranch dressing and chili powder (if desired)

INSTRUCTIONS

1. Bring a large pot of salted water to a boil. Cut the tops off the peppers (or you can leave on for decoration), slice in half the long way, and remove the seeds. Cook peppers in boiling water for 5 minutes; drain. Sprinkle salt inside each pepper, and set aside.
2. In a large skillet cook and brown the ground beef. Once browned, add Maggi's, rice, water and seasonings. Bring to boil, then reduce heat to low, cover, and simmer for 15 – 20 minutes, or until rice is tender.
3. Preheat the oven to 350° Fahrenheit (176° Celsius).
4. Lay the sweet peppers, open side up, in a 9 x 13-inch glass dish.
5. Stuff each pepper with the beef and rice mixture, and top with a heavy sprinkling of cheddar cheese. Bake covered with aluminum foil for 25 to 35 minutes, until heated through and cheese is melted and bubbly (I like to take foil off towards end of baking to let the cheese brown a bit).
6. To garnish (if desired): Drizzle ranch dressing and sprinkle chili powder over each stuffed pepper.

Jen's Italian Meatballs

These are the perfect Italian flavor to me – they are wonderful in pasta sauce, sliced on a pizza, or in a meatball sandwich on my No-Knead Rustic Bread.

Makes: 30 medium sized balls

INGREDIENTS

- 1 pound ground beef
- 1 egg
- 1/2 cup breadcrumbs
- 1/2 cup finely ground parmesan cheese
- 1 teaspoon salt
- 1 teaspoon Italian seasoning
- 1 teaspoon black pepper
- onion salt (more than a few shakes)
- garlic salt (more than a few shakes)
- oregano (more than a few shakes)
- 2 tablespoons freshly chopped basil
- 2 tablespoons freshly chopped cilantro
- 1 tablespoon freshly chopped rosemary
- 1/4 teaspoon cayenne pepper
- 1 teaspoon Worcestershire sauce (yes, you can get this in Costa Rica!)
- 1 teaspoon extra virgin olive oil

INSTRUCTIONS

1. Preheat the oven to 375° Fahrenheit (190° Celsius).
2. Prepare a baking sheet by lining with parchment paper or silicone mat.
3. In a large mixing bowl, combine all ingredients. Mix well, but do not over mix or you will have tough meatballs.
4. Depending on the size you want your meatballs (I usually make mine about a tablespoons worth of meat), portion out meat and place on baking sheet. After all meatballs have been scooped onto tray, roll into balls.
5. Bake for 20-25 minutes. Watch and test; timing depends on your meatball size. They will be brown and sizzling when done. Cut into one to see if it is done. Of course, then you get to taste it too.
6. Remove and transfer to sauce or serve immediately. Can be store in sealed container in the fridge until you are ready to use as well.

6. SWEETS

Coconut and Almond Candy Bars

The joy of almonds and coconuts together! These are my Mom's favorites – especially if dipped in dark chocolate.

Servings: 20

INGREDIENTS

- 4 tablespoons **leche condensada** (USA substitution = sweetened condensed milk)
- 1/2 cup powdered sugar
- 1/2 tablespoon vanilla extract
- pinch of salt
- 1 1/4 cup coconut flakes – unsweetened (or more)
- almonds
- 8 ounces semi-sweet or bittersweet (good quality) chocolate for melting
- 1 teaspoon vegetable shortening (this helps the chocolate to be shiny and less thick after it dries)

INSTRUCTIONS

1. To roast almonds, preheat oven to 350° Fahrenheit (176° Celsius). Spread almonds on a cookie sheet and bake for 10 minutes.
2. In a medium bowl, whisk together *leche condensada*, powdered sugar, salt and vanilla extract. Stir in the unsweetened coconut. Add more coconut if needed – you want a consistency that is pretty thick and will stick together when shaped with your hands.
3. Line a baking sheet with parchment paper (or my favorite, a silicone baking mat). With your hands, shape one tablespoon of coconut mixture into a little log, and press an almond on top. I like to do bite-size, but you can certainly make candy bar size as well. Place the baking sheet in the freezer for 30-45 minutes.
4. Melt chocolate and vegetable shortening in double boiler. Dip the candies in the melted chocolate.
5. Let dipped candy harden in the fridge for 45 minutes. Store in an airtight container at room temperature. If you need to layer the candy in a container, use wax paper to separate the layers.

Peanut Butter Balls

If you like Reese's Peanut Butter Cups – you'll love these.

Makes: 40 balls

INGREDIENTS

- 1 cup peanut butter
- 4 tablespoons butter (cut into small chunks)
- 2 cups powdered sugar (or less)
- 8 ounces semi-sweet or bittersweet (good quality) chocolate for melting
- 1 teaspoon vegetable shortening (this helps the chocolate to be shiny and less thick after it dries)
- peanuts, chopped (for topping)

INSTRUCTIONS

1. In a microwave safe bowl, melt peanut butter and butter together at half power, and watch it – you don't want too liquid-y, but you want both to start melting so you can easily mix them together until smooth.
2. Once smoothly mixed together, add powdered sugar a bit at a time, until correct consistency. NOTE: you may not use all of the powdered sugar. You want a very thick consistency, not too sticky, not too soft, as you will need to roll into balls.
3. Form balls with hands; put on baking sheet with a silicone mat (or parchment or waxed paper). Freeze until hard (30 - 45 minutes).
4. Melt chocolate and vegetable shortening in a double boiler. Dip balls in chocolate, set on another silicone mat on a baking sheet, and sprinkle chopped peanuts on top of each before chocolate sets. Refrigerate to set (30 minutes). Store the candies in a sealed container in the refrigerator, with a guard dog in front of, so your husband doesn't eat them all.

Chocolate Truffle Balls

If you don't tell anyone there are cookies in these, they'll think it's pure decadent chocolate. These are so easy and always get rave reviews!

Makes: 40 balls

INGREDIENTS

- 36 chocolate sandwich cookies (I prefer the OREO® brand)
- 8 ounces **queso crema** (USA substitution = cream cheese), softened
- 2 cups semi-sweet chocolate chips (or other good quality chocolate)
- 1 teaspoon vegetable shortening (this helps the chocolate to be shiny and less thick after it dries)
- 2 – 3 tablespoons white frosting (canned frosting works best)

INSTRUCTIONS

1. Break whole cookies into a food processor, and process until they turn into fine crumbs.
2. Mix cookies and softened *queso crema* together until well blended. Place bowl in freezer for 20-30 minutes.
3. Take a small spoonful of the cookie mixture and shape into a small ball with the palms of your hands. Place on wax paper (or silicone mat) on cookie sheet. Freeze for an hour.
4. Melt chocolate and vegetable shortening in a double boiler.
5. Dip the balls in the chocolate and place on wax paper (or silicone mat) to set.
6. Melt white frosting in microwave at half power until the desired consistency is reached (you do NOT want it too runny). Put into a small plastic sandwich bag, snip the end, and drizzle over the dipped balls. Keep refrigerated until ready to eat.

Turtles

Yes, there are lots of turtles you can see here in Costa Rica, hatching out of their eggs and making their way to the ocean – it's an awesome sight to behold. However, these are the edible kind of turtle – what could be better than caramel, pecans and chocolate? Huge shout out to my pal Bev, for first sharing this recipe with me many moons ago!

Servings: 50

INGREDIENTS:

- 1 package of **Kramel Leche** (USA substitution: 12 – 14 ounces square caramels, individually wrapped)
- 3 tablespoons **leche evaporada** (USA substitution: evaporated milk)
- 2 cups (or more) pecans, halved
- 2 cups semi sweet chocolate chips (or other good quality chocolate)
- 1 tablespoon of vegetable shortening

INSTRUCTIONS:

1. If your pecans are not roasted, please take the time to roast them. It will make a difference; trust me. It's easy – spread pecans on a large cookie sheet and bake at 350° Fahrenheit (176° Celsius) for 5-8 minutes. Let cool.
2. Heat caramels and *leche evaporada* together in a double boiler (or microwave together on half power) until caramels are melted and smooth when mixed. Stir in pecans until fully coated, and drop by spoonfuls on buttered/sprayed wax paper (or silicone mat). Cool in fridge.
3. In clean double boiler, melt chocolate and shortening over low heat until melted. Dip pecan/caramel candies in chocolate with toothpicks or forks and drop onto clean wax paper. Cool in fridge. Once hardened, turtles can be stored at room temperature.

Chocolate Cookie Mini-Cheesecakes

What could be cuter than mini cheesecakes? These are just as good as a whole cheesecake, but you don't even have to slice them. Party perfect.

Servings: 12

INGREDIENTS

Crust
- 10 chocolate sandwich cookies (I prefer the OREO® brand)
- 1 tablespoon unsalted butter, melted

Filling
- 12 ounces **queso crema** (USA substitution = cream cheese), softened
- ½ cups granulated sugar
- 1 teaspoon vanilla
- 1 egg
- 5 chocolate sandwich cookies, coarsely chopped

Whipped cream
- **crema dulce,** refrigerated (USA substitution = refrigerated heavy whipping cream)
- vanilla (to taste)
- powdered sugar (to taste)
- 3 chocolate sandwich cookies (filling removed, each chocolate wafer half cut in half again)

INSTRUCTIONS

1. Preheat oven to 350° Fahrenheit (176° Celsius). Lightly grease a mini cheesecake pan. Set aside.
2. Blend 10 cookies in food processor until only fine crumbs remain. Add melted butter, mix well. Divide among prepared cheesecake cavities. Press down to create a flat crust. Bake for 5 minutes.
3. Reduce oven temperature to 325° Fahrenheit (162° Celsius).
4. In a large bowl or stand mixer, beat cream cheese with sugar until smooth. Add in vanilla, egg and the cookie pieces. Mix until just combined. Fill each cheesecake pan cavity 3/4 full. Use spoon to smooth out and fill in any air pockets.
5. Bake for 25-27 minutes, turning halfway through. Use a toothpick to check for doneness. (You want the toothpick to come out cake-y, not liquid-y.) Cool completely on a wire rack. Transfer to fridge to chill at least 4 hours or overnight.
6. To make whipped cream, put mixing bowl and mixing whisk from mixer in freezer for 15 minutes. Add *crema dulce* to mixing bowl, and whip on high speed until stiff peaks form. Add vanilla and powdered sugar to taste. Carefully remove cheesecakes from pan, removing pan bottoms. Top off with whipped cream (I put in plastic sandwich bag and cut a good size whole in the tip to make a very thick swirl) and half of a cookie. Store cheesecakes in the refrigerator.

A WORD ABOUT FOOD IN COSTA RICA

Costa Rica, being a foreign country and all, has some differences compared to the United States. You might say, "Well, duh," but many expatriates here seem to be surprised by this. Let's discuss some of the food anomalies in Costa Rica.

WHERE TO BUY FOOD:

From my experience, living in the small town of Grecia in the Central Valley, we have three different types of places to purchase food.

First of all, the average grocery store is much smaller than in the States and has fewer choices; however, they have most everything you will need (paper products, cleaning supplies, toiletries, canned goods, cookies/breads, ice cream, sodas and alcohol). Most grocery stores will have a butcher department, refrigerated dairy section, and a small frozen section (you will pay much higher prices for pre-packaged/frozen meal items, as they are mostly exported from the States). A few names of grocery stores to look for in Grecia: *Peri* (small grocery store downtown), *Pali* (small store, discount products, much like ALDI in the States), *Rosvil* (small but comprehensive grocery store downtown), *Super Rosvil* (the largest grocery store in Grecia, located behind the feria exit by the tribunal building), and *Maxi Pali* (similar to a small Walmart in the States with a decent grocery section). *AutoMercado*, a chain of grocery stores found in larger towns (not Grecia) and owned by a gringo, has many items the average gringo wants but can't find; but of course, they come at a higher price. A large warehouse type store similar to Costco or Sam's Club and also found in larger towns is *PriceSmart*. You have to have a membership card to find both good deals (for hard-to-find gringo products) and not-so-good deals. I've compared prices on items you can also find in regular grocery stores, and even though you can find larger quantities at *PriceSmart,* it is more expensive than if you bought the same quantity in smaller packages at a regular grocery store.

Secondly, there are the markets. Each city tends to have its own farmers' market (called the "*feria*"), and Grecia's is topnotch. They have a permanent area set aside for use on Fridays and Saturdays. There are rows and rows of farmers with their booths set up with fresh vegetables and fruits. Other booths include organic vegetables, refrigerated meats, cheese, coffee and even some non-food items like trinkets and clothes. Grecia's *feria* also has a couple of *sodas* (small cafes) set up in the middle where you can purchase *batidos* (fresh fruit drinks) or something to eat. At the *feria* you can get a plethora of fresh vegetables and fruit at really good prices.

Another type of market is the "central market" (*mercado central*) – which is located in the downtown area of larger towns. These indoor markets with permanent booths are typically open every day except Sunday. You can find things like fresh vegetables and fruit, meat and other things like baking supplies, containers, plastic bags, pots & pans, *etc*. If you're looking for something, go to the *mercado central* and walk around. Chances are you'll find it.

And finally, a third type of place to buy food in many towns is a store that specializes in produce (in Grecia the store is called *La Gran Bodega*). It is usually a stand-alone store, and the majority of what it carries is fresh vegetables and fruits. They also typically have really good chicken, beef and fish. Sometimes you can find items here that you cannot even find at the *feria* (*i.e., jalapeños)* and the prices are very reasonable. They normally have a few aisles of grocery store type items (chips, canned goods, toiletries), but the selection is minimal.

BAG OR BOX:

One small difference in Costa Rica versus the States is there are a lot of liquid items that come in either a bag or a 1-liter box (vs. a jug, carton or bottle). Examples of bags: *natilla* (really more like *crème fraîche*, but this is the closest thing Costa Rica has to sour cream), salad dressing, mayonnaise, and catsup. Examples of 1-liter boxes: boxed wine (which is actually very good), juices, and milk. You will also find liquid milk in the aisle of a grocery store (non-refrigerated) which has been vacuum sealed and is actually fine to store on a shelf; just watch the expiration date on top. Once opened, refrigerate, and it lasts about a week after you have opened it. *Crema dulce* comes in a 1-liter box (or a very small box, 250 ml, which is about 1 cup).

A word about *crema dulce* – this is what I use in Costa Rica in place of cream, and I like the Dos Pinos brand. The only way I have found to obtain REAL cream is from the milkman, who actually gets it from a dairy close by. He gives you raw milk straight from the cow, and after sitting in your fridge, the cream will rise to the top. However, it can be hard to catch the milkman if you're not on a weekly schedule, and the boxed *crema dulce* is readily available in all grocery stores. *Crema dulce* has a 35% fat content and works in two different ways:

1. You store it in your pantry at room temperature. It is vacuum-sealed so you can store on your shelf, and like the milk, you need to pay attention to the expiration date on the top. You can use *crema dulce* for any soup that calls for cream (like my recipe for Tomato Basil Soup), and it is perfect for making them creamier and thicker. Also this is good for making an alfredo sauce for pasta.

2. You can also store it in your refrigerator and use to make whipped cream topping (like Cool Whip). The trick is to have your stainless steel mixing bowl and beaters in the freezer for 30 minutes or more, pour in the cold *crema dulce*, and whip. You will need to add sweetener and vanilla to taste, but this makes a delicious whipped cream. NOTE: It will NOT whip if it has not been refrigerated.

RESTAURANTS IN COSTA RICA:

There are tons of small cafes called *sodas* in Costa Rica that are actually all very good. A soda is a mom-and-pop type of restaurant. They usually have just a few tables or booths, and you can also get food "to go" (HINT: *"para llevar, por favor"* is what you say to the wait staff if you want something to go). They serve very typical Costa Rican food. The larger places are called restaurants and are more what we are used to in the States, sit-down places where you will be waited on, and they usually have beer and sometimes wine. Service is pretty good, as long as you remember *tico time*. Sometimes you will just need to be patient and wait for things. When you are finished, you usually have to go to the bar area or cash register to pay. It is typical for them to ask you what you had; they will add it up and tell you the total. Most places include a 10% service fee so there is no need to tip. You can look at the bill or receipt to verify this.

A typical Costa Rican dish you can find in most sodas or restaurants is called a *casado*, which is slightly different everywhere, but generally will include your choice of meat (chicken, beef or fish) and comes with rice, beans, sometimes an egg, and avocado, sometimes fried plantain, and sometimes a small salad. It is usually a healthy sized portion although they sometimes offer it in two different sizes (note: the small or *pequeña* is still a hearty size!). Another typical dish is *gallo pinto* (rice and beans), which is very easy to find and mainly served at breakfast – you can order it with meat or eggs or a side of *natilla*. If you are not interested in one of the national beers to wash down your meal, most restaurants of any size offer *batidos*, which are fresh fruit drinks made in a blender with ice and either water or milk. You pick your fruit (they will tell you what they have – usually pineapple, mora berry, cas, strawberry, guanabana, *etc.*), and they blend it for you. It is a delicious and refreshing fruit shake.

We've had so much fun learning about all the differences and nuances with food that make up this little country. There's so much more to learn, but that's why life here is never boring.

A FINAL WORD:

My husband paid me the highest compliment the other day when we learned of a pizza delivery place down the road. He, who *lived* for ordering pizza delivery in the States, after thinking about it for a second, said, "Nah, I wouldn't want to get pizza delivery here. Your homemade pizza is the best!"

Before moving to Costa Rica, I never would have thought I would come to enjoy cooking so much. I love researching different recipes for the same dish, and then mixing and matching different ingredients or measurements to make it my own. The more you do this, the more confidence you will have in yourself and your abilities – especially when the final product is such a hit!

It can be somewhat frustrating cooking in Costa Rica, at least at first, with so many language and cultural differences. I hope this cookbook alleviates some of the pitfalls and frustrations for you.

Now, go pour yourself a glass of boxed wine, get in that kitchen, and START COOKING!

BONUSES

Taco Seasoning

The typical Costa Rican grocery store does not carry those handy-dandy taco seasoning packets. But wait – you can make your own taco seasoning right at home. Try it, you might never go back.

INGREDIENTS

- 1 tablespoon chili powder
- 1 teaspoon ground cumin
- 1 teaspoon garlic powder
- 1 teaspoon paprika
- 1/2 teaspoon oregano
- 1/2 teaspoon onion powder
- 1/4 teaspoon salt
- 1/4 teaspoon black pepper
- ½ teaspoon cayenne pepper or 1/4 teaspoon crushed red pepper flakes
- 1 teaspoon flour (optional)

INSTRUCTIONS

Mix all ingredients together. If using red pepper flakes, process in food processor.

FOR TACO DIP: Mix 2 tablespoons + 1 teaspoon of taco seasoning with 16 ounces of **Del Prado Natilla** (I like this brand the best for this dip, USA substitute = sour cream), spread onto a plate or shallow bowl, top with shredded cheddar cheese. Serve with tortilla chips!

Garlic Parmesan Cheese Bites

These little cheese bites? They are the bomb! They will make strong men go "ooh and ahh" – I guarantee you. Try them – they are a hit at parties, or of course for any time you want to feel just a bit happier.

Makes: about 32 bites

INGREDIENTS

- 1 stick of butter, melted
- 3 cloves of garlic, minced
- 1/2 teaspoon garlic powder
- 1/2 cup grated parmesan cheese
- 1 teaspoon black pepper
- 3 teaspoons Italian seasoning
- block of cheddar cheese, cut into 32 - 1" cubes

INSTRUCTIONS

1. Mix the butter with the garlic cloves and garlic powder, set aside.
2. Mix the parmesan cheese with black pepper and Italian seasoning, set aside.
3. Take about a large (grapefruit size) chunk of my No-Knead Rustic Bread dough (HINT: make sure the No-Knead Dough has been refrigerated before using). I like to make into a *boule* shape, set on a heavily floured surface, sprinkle with flour and cover with a towel for about 20 minutes. Then cut in half with a pastry cutter, and keep cutting in half until you have 32 small chunks of dough.
4. Take one piece of dough and flatten out on a floured surface or in your hands. Stick a cube of cheddar cheese in the middle, shape dough over it to form a ball. Dip in the butter/garlic mixture, and then roll in the parmesan mixture. Place the ball on a baking sheet lined with a silicone mat (or parchment paper) and repeat these steps until you have 32 balls ready to bake.
5. Bake at 400° Fahrenheit (104° Celsius) for 20-22 minutes (should be slightly browned on top and sizzling and your house will smell heavenly!).
6. Serve immediately, while still warm. Enjoy!

NOTE: Play around, experiment! You can do lots of things with the ingredients above, like Garlic Parmesan Bread Sticks…

Garlic Parmesan Bread Sticks

These breadsticks are SO flavorful and yummy.
Excellent for dipping in ANY of my soups. Or just by themselves.

INGREDIENTS

Same ingredients as the Garlic Parmesan Cheese Bites on previous page (except no cheddar cheese).

INSTRUCTIONS

1. Take one piece of dough and roll it into a stick (about 6 inches long). I use my hands and a silicone dough mat, floured, for rolling. Keep your hands floured. Dip in the butter/garlic mixture, and then roll in the parmesan mixture (alternatively, you can brush the butter/garlic mixture just on top and heavily sprinkle with the parmesan mixture).
2. Bake on a baking sheet lined with a silicone mat (or parchment paper) at 400° Fahrenheit (204° Celsius) for 15-18 minutes.
3. You're welcome!

THANKS

THANKS TO YOU, DEAR READER, for purchasing this book. Whether you are a friend, a follower of my blog, or you just found this by chance – I appreciate each and every one of you. You guys keep me going and alive with your positive comments and feedback.

Thanks to Bina Cline and Lynette Hunt for being my "test kitchen" for some of my initial recipes. It helped tremendously to have someone (other than myself) actually making the recipes and offering feedback and critique on measurements, wording, and taste.

Thanks to Lynette Hunt for editing my initial draft. With your red pen, you helped me address several things right off the bat, and I'm very grateful to you. Thank you also for your friendship and enthusiasm whenever I make something new (I love that you always want the recipe!). Also, thanks to you and Mark, for the use of your beautiful kitchen for my cover picture shoot – that was a fun day.

HUGE thanks to Jeni Evans for editing my final product. You amaze me with how many things you bring to my attention, and your grasp of the English language. I honestly don't know where I'd be without you. Thanks for all your explanations and always trying to teach me "better English," but also your patience when I don't seem to remember anything. Don't ever leave me!

Most importantly, thanks to my Greg, for always inspiring me with your affirmative comments whenever I bake or cook. Also for your over the top eagerness whenever I told you I had to make a recipe again and again "for research." You are my most excellent taste tester and encourager. Thanks also for your mad photography and photo shop skills. I couldn't have done this book without you.

If you're wondering about my beautiful Kitchen Aid mixer on the cover, my talented friend Pamela Hopkins painted this while she lived here in Costa Rica. She turned my old generic white mixer into a real work of art with Costa Rican colors, flowers and animals. I love walking into my kitchen every morning and being hit with this beautiful, bright sight. Thank you, Pam!

ABOUT THE AUTHOR

Jen is the author of the bestselling book *Costa Rica Chica*: *Retiring Early, Simplifying My Life, & Realizing That Less is Best.*

When she's not writing or blogging, she is either baking, hiking, playing piano, yoga-ing, sipping coffee, making arm candy or enjoying a glass of (boxed) wine... or yelling at her husband to come save her from a bug.

She lives with her husband near Grecia, Alajuela, Costa Rica.

Follow Jen's adventures at: www.CostaRicaChica.com

27261251R10058

Made in the USA
Middletown, DE
14 December 2015